I0110967

Emerald Isle Sampler

14 ct 101x197 Stitches (18.3 x 35.7 cm) (7.2 x 14.1 in.)

Counted Cross-Stitch Patterns

by CARI BUZIAK

Lil'Llama
Press

Cross-stitch pattern designed by Cari Buziak
© Cari Buziak
Aon-Celtic.com

Emerald Isle Sampler

14 ct 101x197 Stitches
(18.3 x 35.7 cm) (7.2 x 14.1 in.)

		DMC		
C	C	DMC	703	Chartreuse
■	□	DMC	986	Forest Green very dark
⋮	⋮	DMC	3078	Golden Yellow very lt
8	8	DMC	3822	Straw light
❑	❑	DMC	3852	Straw very dark

Backstitching - 2 strands	
——	Backstitching - DMC 3852
——	Backstitching - DMC 703

✤ I usually do two strands when backstitching these sort of designs, where the stitches make designs, so they show up better. But feel free to do 1 strand if it's too heavy for your taste.

Emerald Isle Sampler

Emerald Isle Sampler

Emerald Isle Sampler

Emerald Isle Sampler

Emerald Isle Sampler

Emerald Isle Sampler

Emerald Isle Sampler

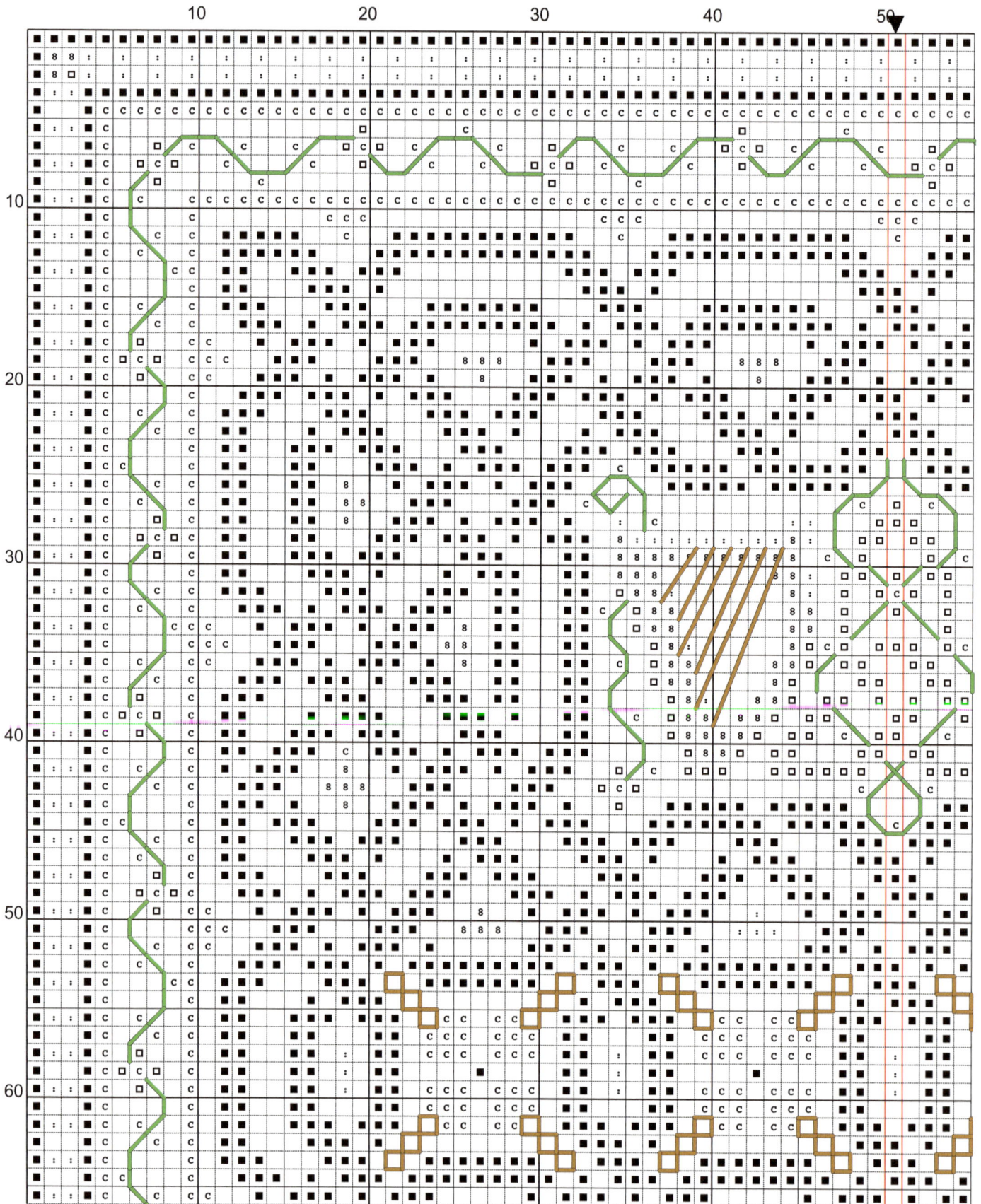

Emerald Isle Sampler

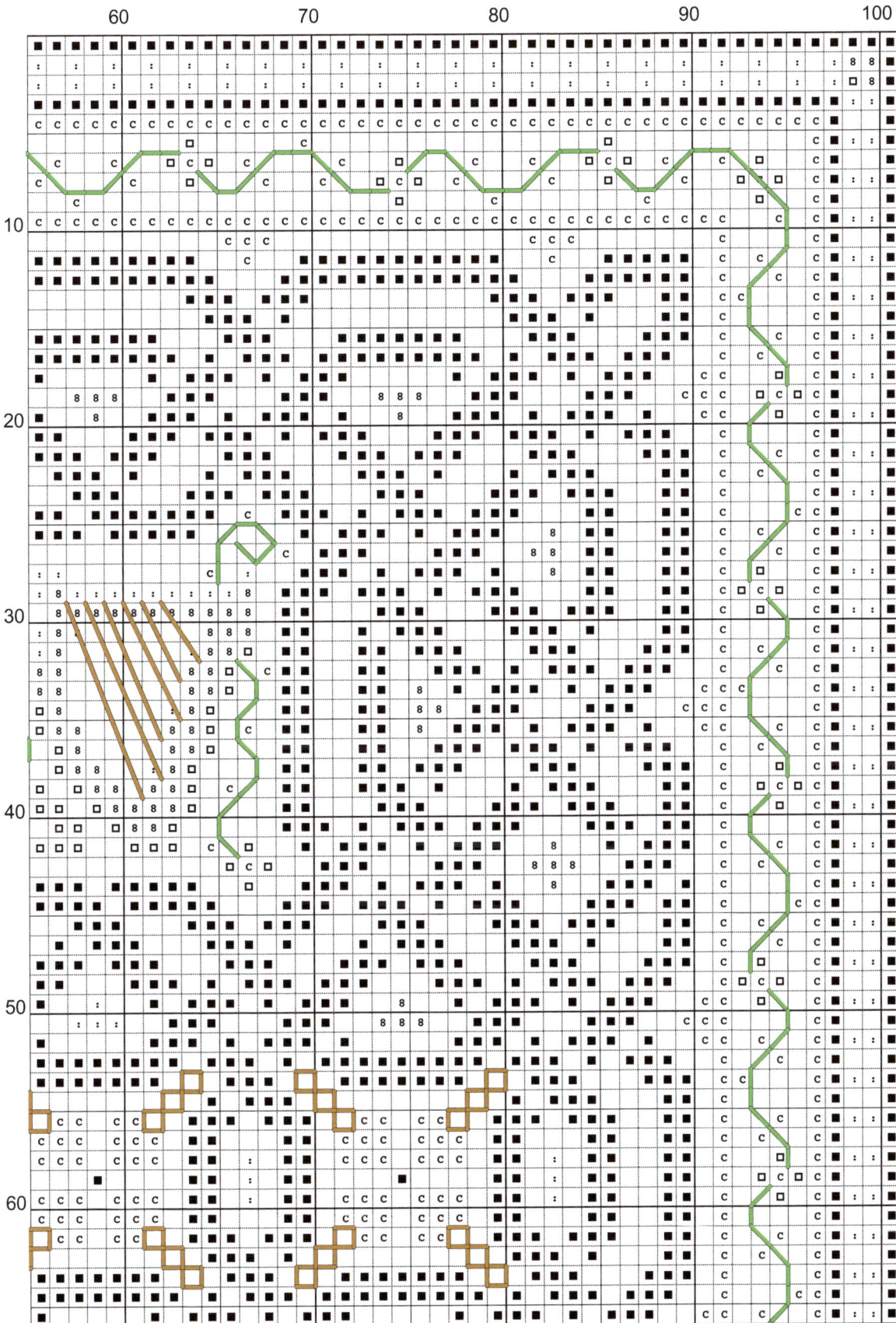

Emerald Isle Sampler

Emerald Isle Sampler

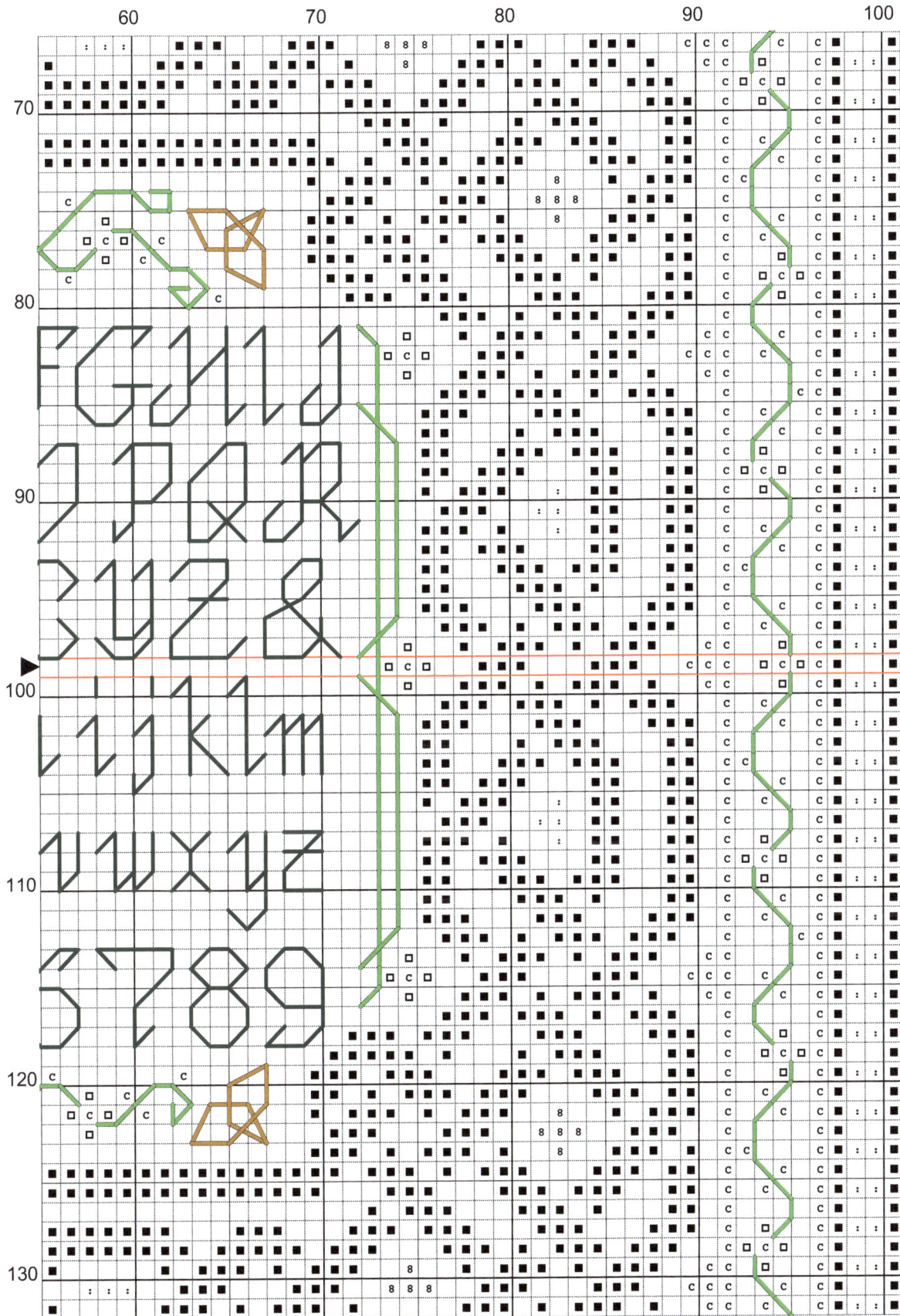

Emerald Isle Sampler

Emerald Isle Sampler

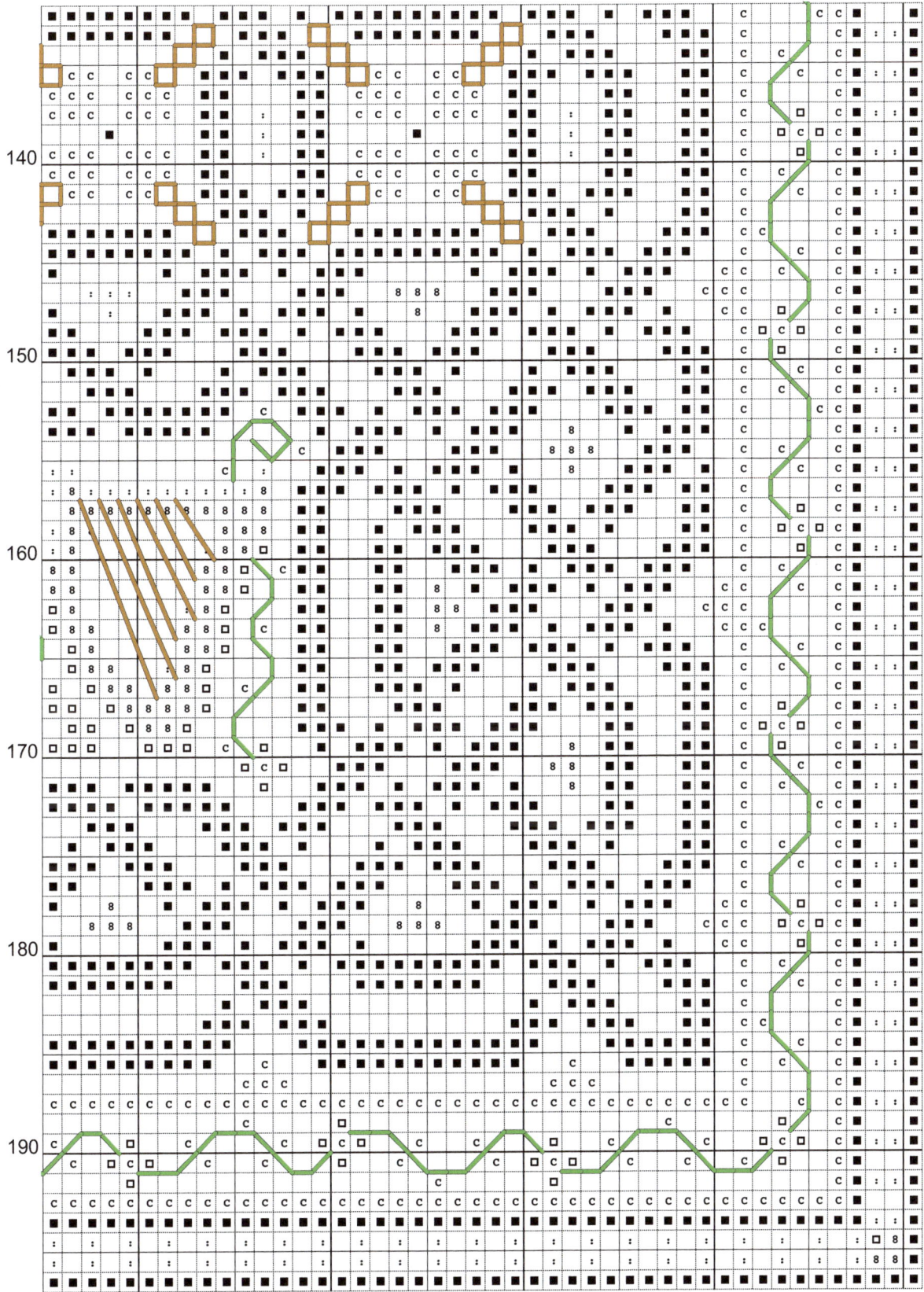

Emerald Isle Sampler

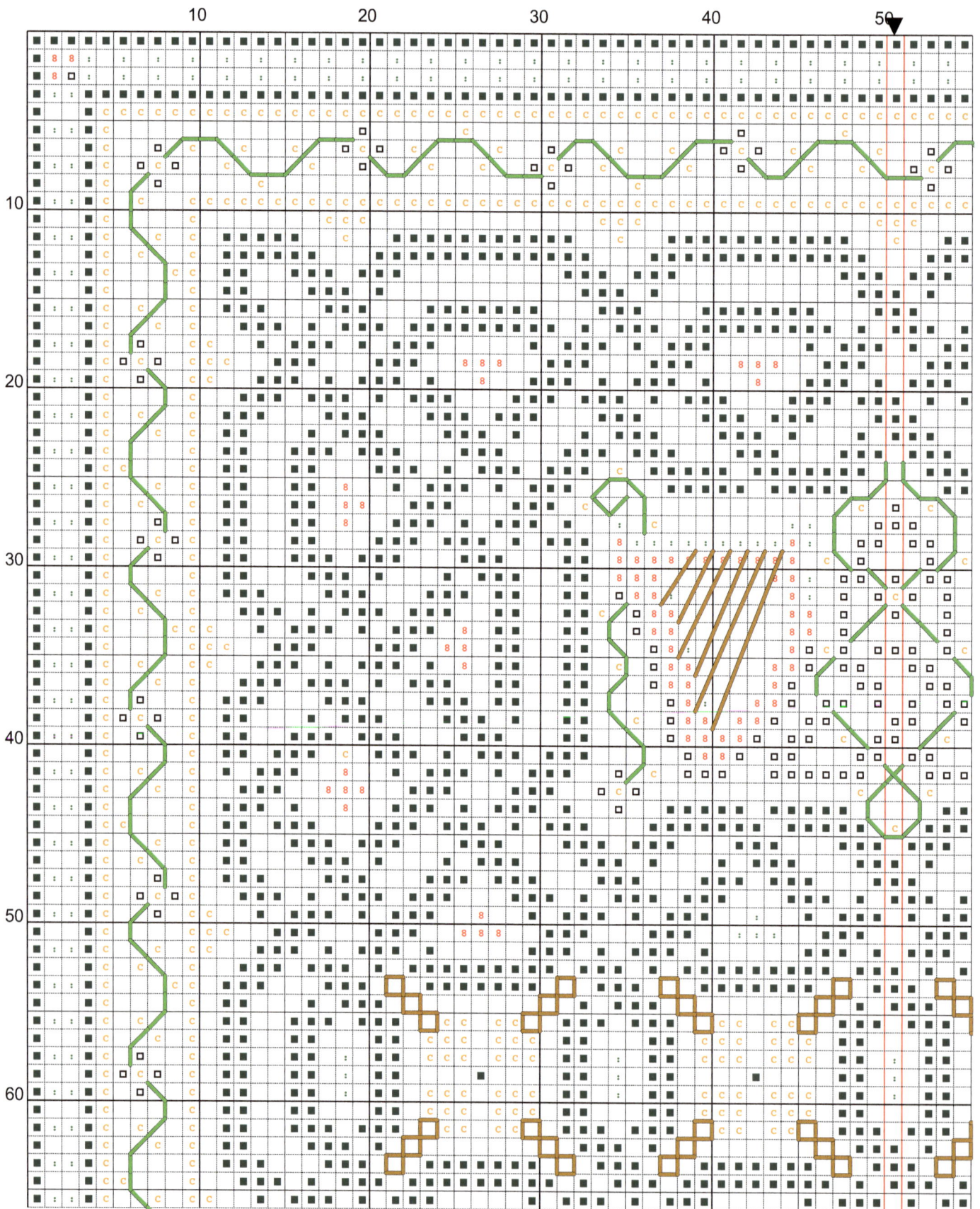

Emerald Isle Sampler

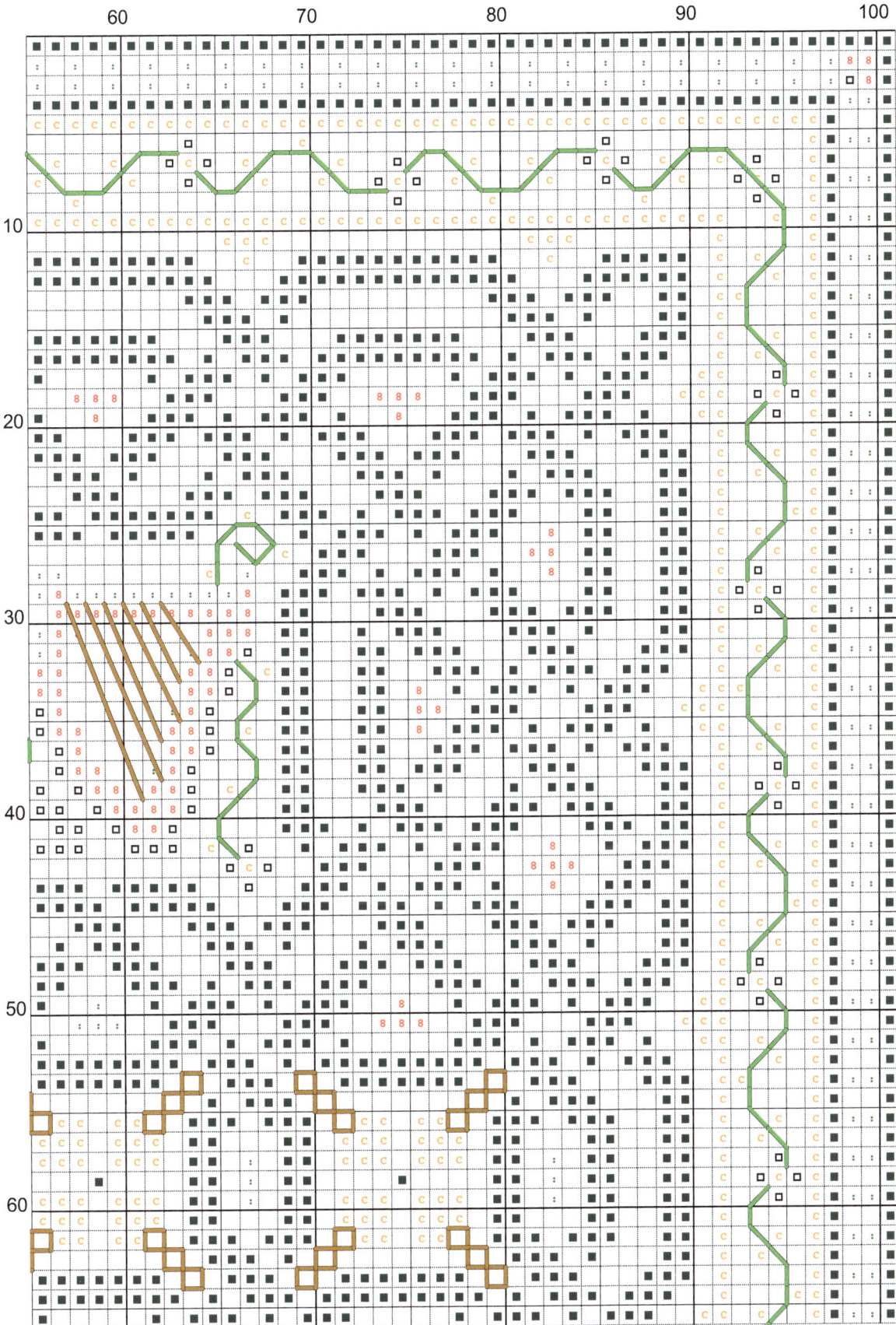

Emerald Isle Sampler

Emerald Isle Sampler

Emerald Isle Sampler

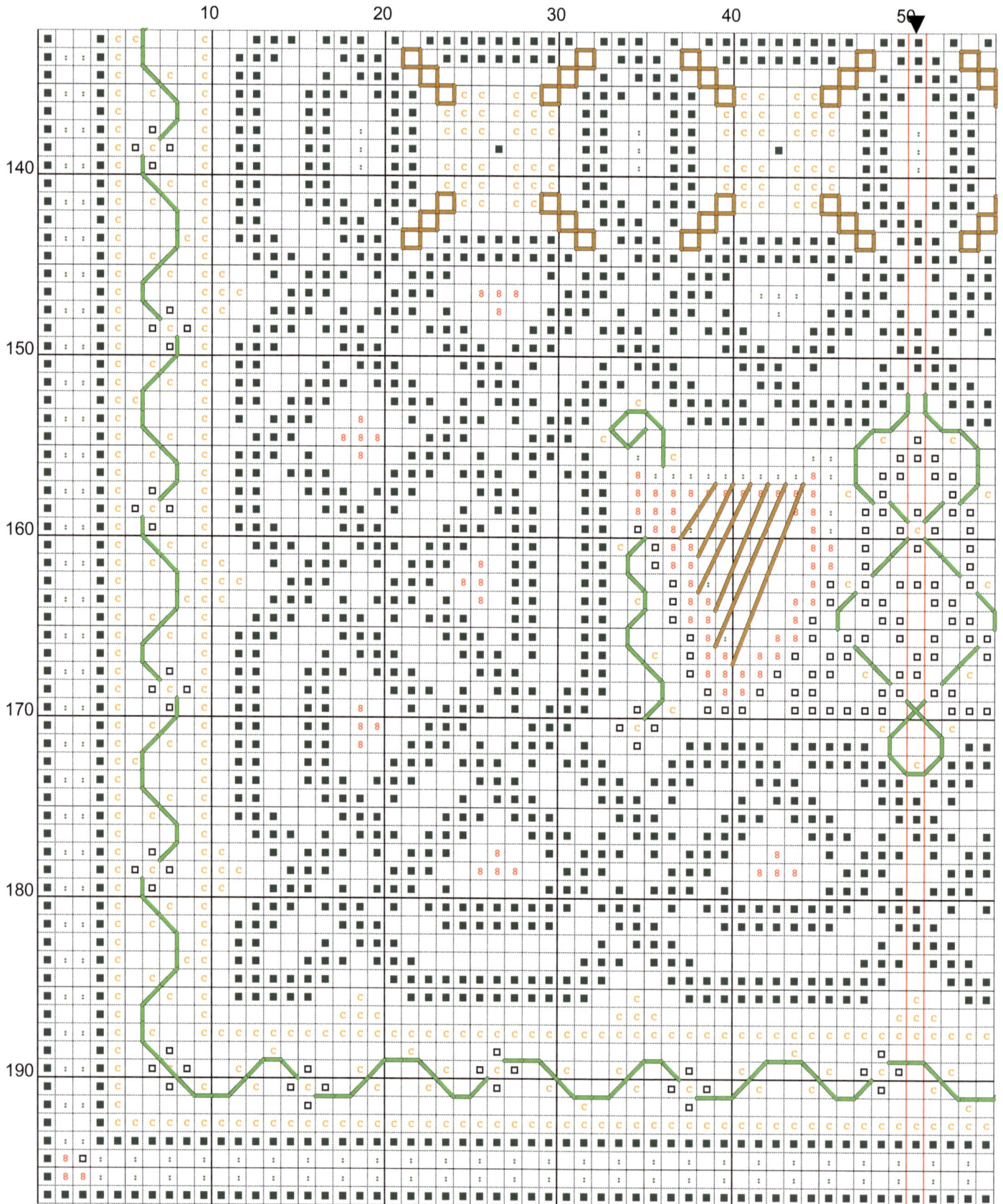

Emerald Isle Sampler

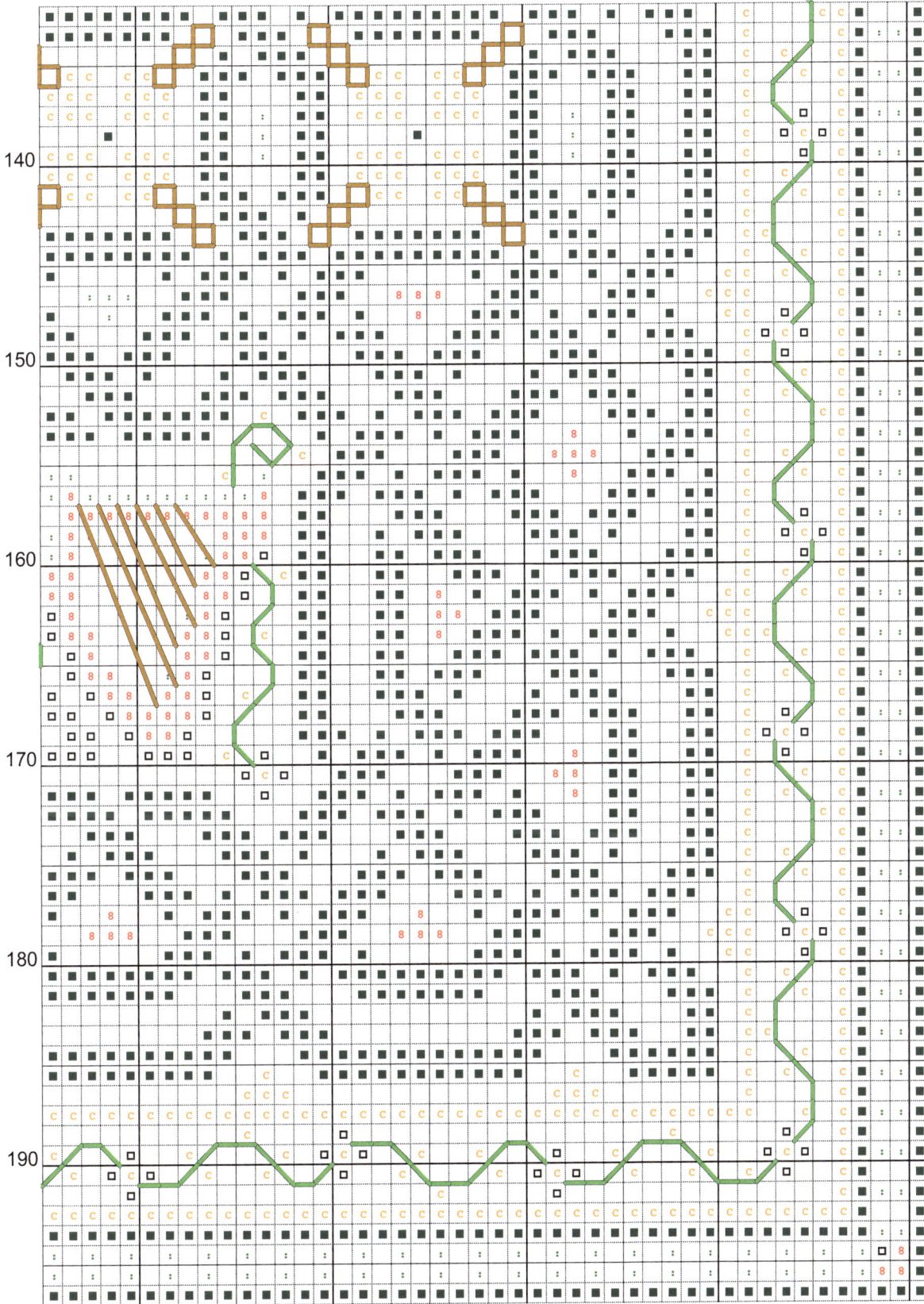

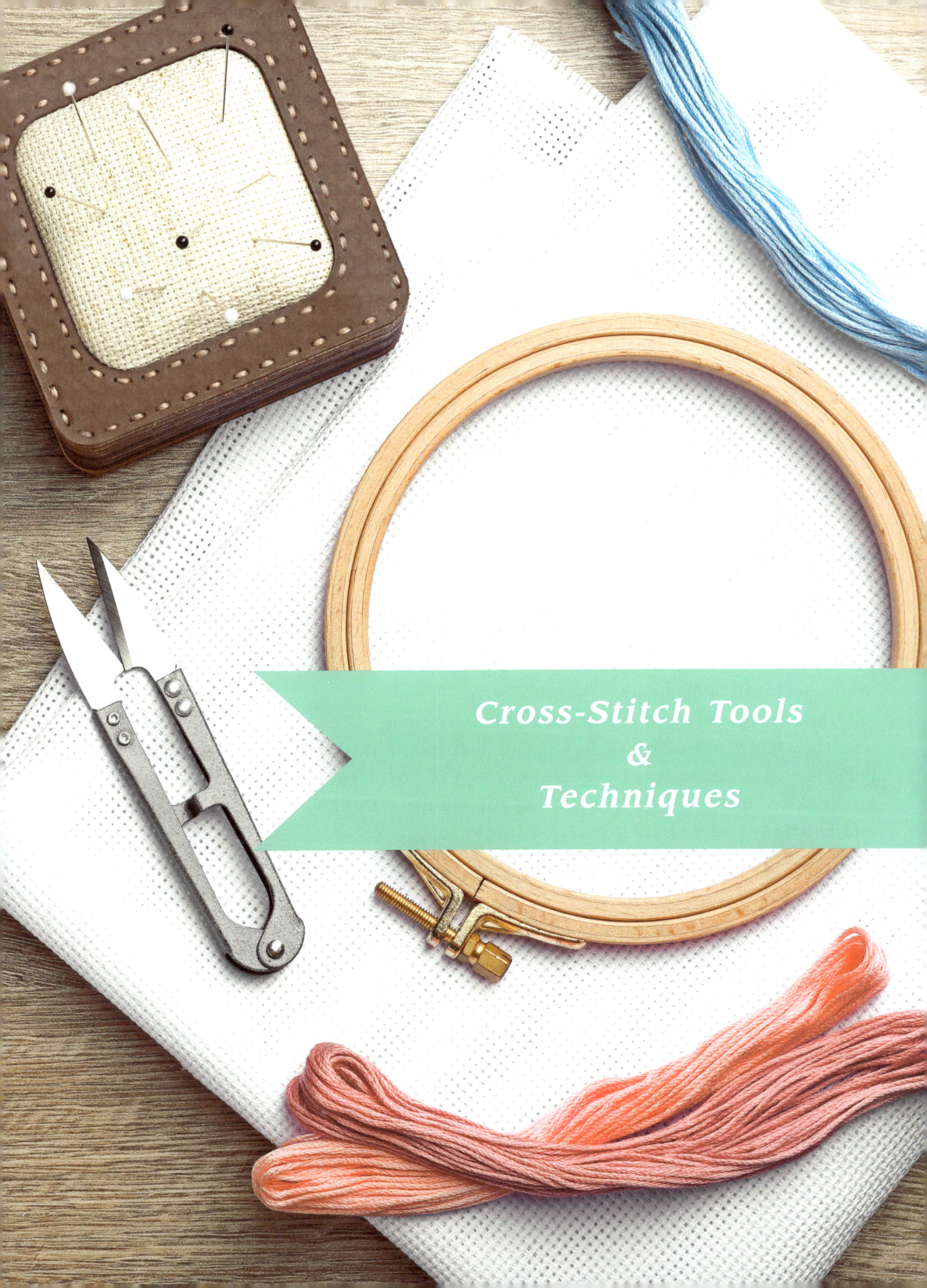

Cross-Stitch Tools
&
Techniques

Cross-Stitch Tools & Techniques

History

People have been decorating their tools and possessions for thousands of years. The earliest pieces of embroidery were found in the late 1800's within an Egyptian tomb, which dated the piece to approximately 500AD. Crossed-over stitches were in use (along with other techniques, such as couching, chain stitching, and backstitching) and eventually become its own identifiable technique between 1100 and 1500AD in the states of Islam. During the 1500's it was brought to England, where it gained in popularity – leading to the first counted cross-stitch pattern books being published!

Bayeux Tapestry, 11th century, Bayeux Museum

Traditionally, cross-stitch was used to decorate and personalize household items such as linen, table clothes, and clothing. Samplers were created and shared as a way to feature the skills of the stitcher and to make examples of commonly stitched shapes and patterns, such as letters and other decorative elements. The stitcher only had to refer to their "sampler" when stitching a new piece of work to reference how they had stitched the design in the past. While this embroidery technique has had periods of ups and downs in its use, during the Covid-19 pandemic cross-stitching saw an uptake of interest from the crafting community – along with baking sourdough bread and knitting. Truly, no craft ever gets old!

Today cross-stitch is enjoyed by the young and old, men and women, all around the world. Computer programs and apps are used to create and share charts, and to aid in stitching. It is truly a craft that knows no bounds!

Stitching Surface

The most common type of cloth to stitch on is called *Aida cloth*, which can be purchased at any craft store. The strands of this fabric are grouped in pairs so the it's very easy to see where each 'X' of your cross-stitch should go and makes it a great cloth for beginners to learn on. *Evenweave cloth* can be any cloth with a coarse weave to it, such as linen or "luganda" cloth. Any of these fabrics can be found in an array of colors, or you can experiment with hand dying them particular shades with colorfast fabric dyes or tea.

Your stitching surface doesn't even have to be cloth! Anything with an even weave can be used – try searching online for examples of cross-stitch on window screens or even kitchen sieves!

Your cross-stitch pattern should have the finished size of the project noted in its basic information. Make sure your chosen fabric is at least 6-8″ larger than the project size. This will give you at least 3″ all around your design to hold the fabric in your hand or mount it in a hoop while you stitch, and for framing when it's finished. Remember – you can always trim excess off later, but you can't add more on!

Aida Cloth

Evenweave Cloth

Needles

You need a special needle for cross-stitching, called a tapestry needle. This needle has a larger eye and a blunt tip, which finds its way between the strands of your fabric easily. Traditional pointed needles may pierce or split the threads of your cloth, and will be much harder to stitch with.

Embroidery Floss

Cross-stitch patterns have at least two parts – a *chart*, showing the design in a grid-like layout, and a *key* to the chart, showing the symbols that appeared in the chart and the colors assigned to them. The colors are numbered by the manufacturer (DMC or Anchor usually), and sometimes by the color name. To complete a cross-stitch pattern you'll need to purchase a skein of each color listed in the key. Usually you'll need only one skein of each color, but if you need more the key will usually say so. To keep your floss tidy and organized, many stitchers will wind the floss around cardboard bobbins and write the color number on the bobbin. Special cases can be found in craft stores to store your bobbins neatly.

DMC floss numbers are provided with each stitch key in this book, as well as the Anchor equivalent. Not all DMC colors have an equivalent in the Anchor system, so be sure to double check your colors if you're using Anchor threads, especially if the pattern calls for a smooth transition between colors or shades, like a gradient.

Finding Center

To make sure that your project is centered on your fabric, you'll need to find the center. Fold your fabric in half, side to side. Then fold it in half again, top to bottom. The fabric should now be in quarters. Mark the center with a temporary stitch or a pin.

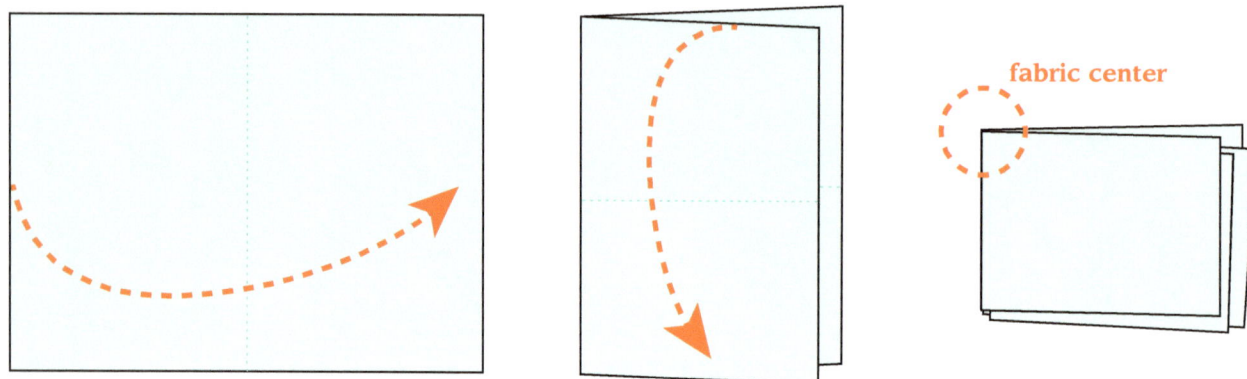

fabric center

Your chart should have arrows at the edges that will help you find the center of the design. Simply follow those arrows from the horizontal and the vertical, and where they meet will be the center of the design. You may want to mark that place with a small pencil dot on your chart.

To keep track of your stitching, it's helpful to work from a photocopy that you can mark up with a highlighter or colored pencil, coloring the completed squares as you go. The grid of your chart will usually have a darker line every ten squares, and some stitchers will stitch a long basting stitch of any color on their fabric to correspond with those lines on the chart. If you have a large project, this can really help to make sure you don't lose your place! There's also an app called *PatternKeeper* that a lot of stitchers use to keep track of their progress. Visit their website below to learn more about their app and how you can use it with your projects:

PatternKeeper: www.patternkeeper.app

Flossing the Needle

Embroidery floss comes wrapped in skeins, and each skein is made up of six individual strands of floss. Your pattern will tell you how many strands of floss to use for the cross-stitching, and how many to use for the backstitching, but usually you'll stitch with two strands for cross-stitching and a single strand for backstitching. If you're stitching on darker colors, or prefer stronger color to your stitches, you can try stitching with three strands for the cross-stitches and two for the backstitching instead. Just keep in mind that you'll go through more thread if you're using more strands of thread, so for colors that are used a lot you may need an extra skein of floss.

To begin, cut about 18-24" of thread from the skein, and then use your fingers separate one strand from the others. Pulling the threads out one by one from the skein is a little more time consuming, but it'll keep the thread from becoming tangled while you stitch and will also help your stitches lay flat. Pull out one strand, and then pull out another strand, until you have as many as you need or want to stitch with. Leave the rest of the strands together until you need them and rewind them on the bobbin for safe-keeping.

Now take your two pulled strands and put them together, and thread your needle. *But don't knot the end of your thread!*

Starting & Finishing Stitching

Cross-stitchers don't use knots to fasten the ends of the threads. This would cause unsightly bumps to show through from the back of the fabric. To fasten the ends of the thread so your work doesn't unravel, leave a 1" tail of thread on the backside of the fabric when you pull your needle through for the first stitch. Come up from the bottom, leaving your 1" tail behind, and then go back down through the front of the fabric in the appropriate hole (see below). When you come back up to start the other half of that first stitch, take care to make sure that the loop in the back catches the tail you left, so that when the thread is pulled tight the tail is secured by the loop. After a few stitches like this, the tail should be held snugly in place, and any excess tail can be trimmed away.

Stitch until you're down to about 3" of thread, or until you need to make a color change. At the end of your last stitch, turn the work over and use your needle to weave the thread through the back of a few stitches, until it looks secure. Trim the remaining thread.

During the course of stitching, you may find that your thread becomes twisted and wants to knot up. To fix this, occasionally let go of your needle as you stitch and let it hang to unwind.

Cross-Stitch Basics

Cross-stitching involves making a series of X's in your fabric. Whether you're stitching on Aida cloth or evenweave cloth, the basics of stitching your X is the same. The only difference is that the Aida cloth has the strands "clumped" in twos, which makes it really easy to see where to insert your needle. On evenweave cloth, commonly you'll stitch over two strands of cloth at a time, and you just have to make sure you keep all your X's in the same row, horizontally and vertically.

Regardless of what cloth you're stitching on, an important rule in cross-stitching is to make sure that the topmost stitch lays in the same direction across your whole project!

To begin stitching, follow the steps below:

Step 1 - Come up through hole 1, go down in hole 2

Step 2 - Come back up in hole 3, go down in hole 4

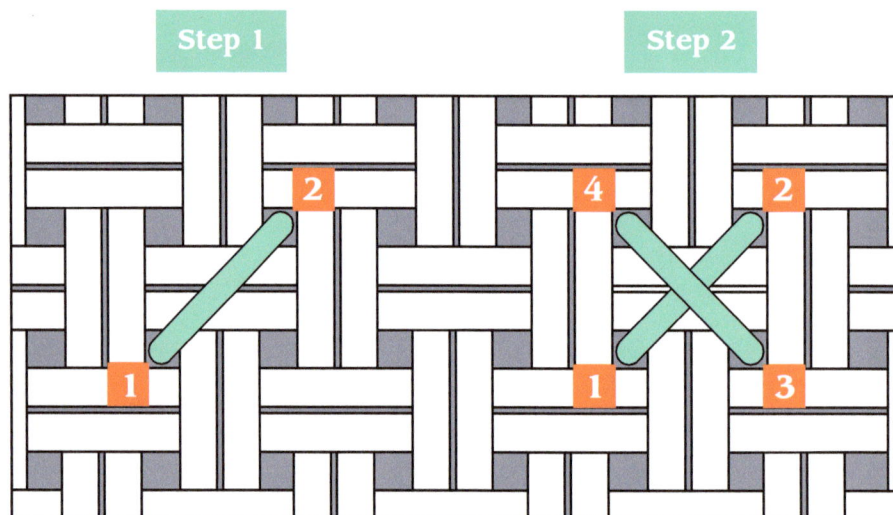

Aida Cloth

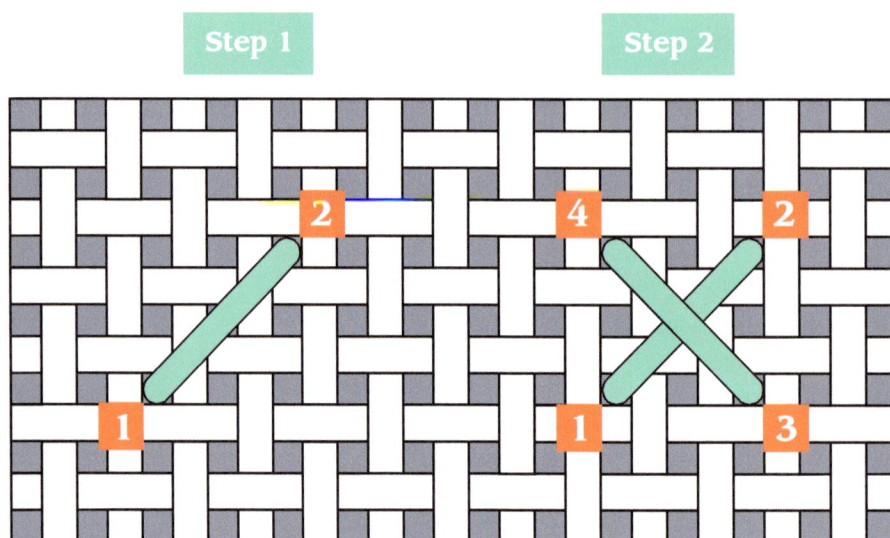

Evenweave Cloth

Multiple Stitches

If you have a lot of stitches in the same color, you can complete them quickly by using the following technique. Basically, you make the first stitch in one direction as many times as needed. Afterwards, you work backwards to "cross them off" in the other direction!

Step 1 - Come up through hole 1, go down in hole 2, up through hole 3, down in hole 4, and so on.

Step 2 - Come up through hole A, go down in hole B, up through hole C, down in D, etc.

Aida Cloth

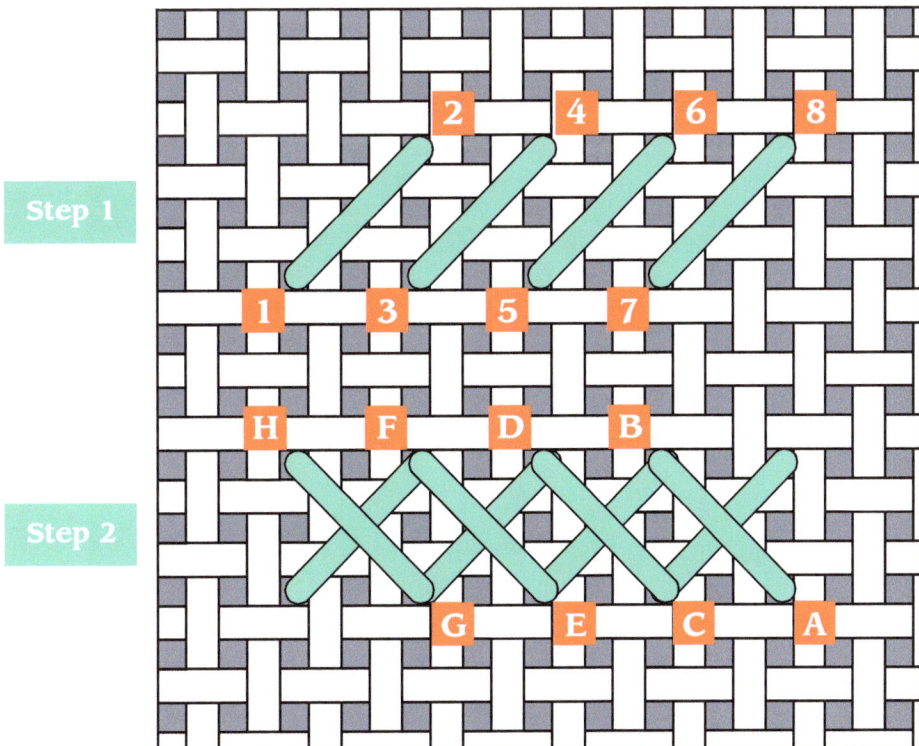

Evenweave Cloth

Partial Stitches

All the patterns in this book use whole stitches. But some patterns may call for partial stitches, which can smooth or round out a design along the edge or where colors meet. The quadrant where the 1/4 or 3/4 stitch occurs will be shown in the pattern. Some patterns can call for stitches using one thread in two different colors, stitched together to give a "blended" look or to smooth a transition between two colors.

If you're looking for more cross-stitch techniques, visit the *RSN StitchBank online*. They have illustrations and instructions on a wealth of needlepoint techniques and the history behind them, including cross-stitch:

RSN StitchBank: www.rsnstitchbank.org, and www.rsnstitchbank.org/stitch/cross-stitch

Lord Libidan's website is also a great resource: https://lordlibidan.com

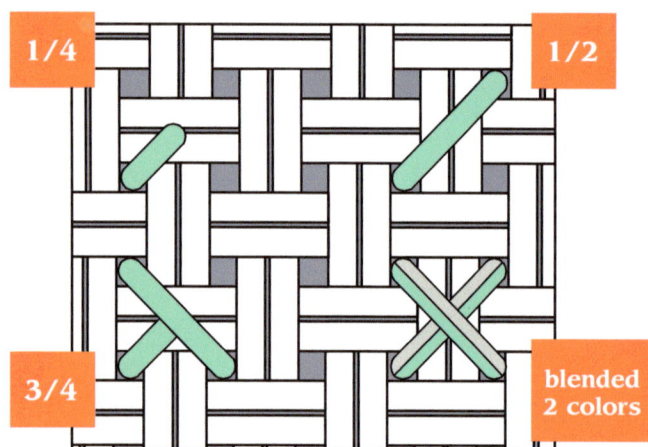

Aida Cloth

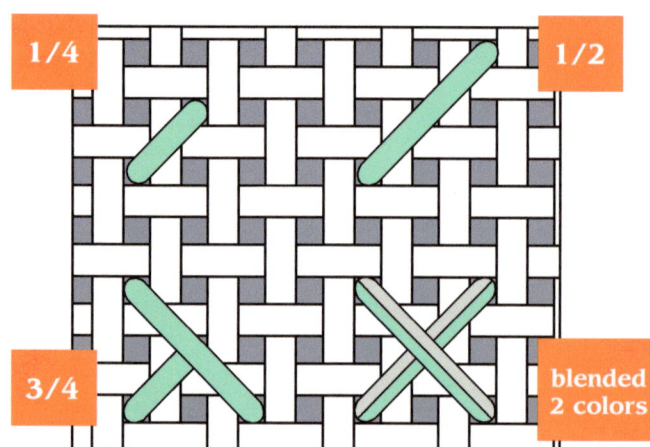

Evenweave Cloth

Backstitching

Backstitching is done when you've completed your entire pattern. This step really brings the whole project into focus, and is used to define edges, colors, and to add fine details. Your pattern key will tell you what color is needed for the backstitches, and how many threads to use (usually one or two).

Backstitches form a continuous line of stitches. They're made by inserting the needle in a kind of staggered approach through the fabric.

Step 1 - Come up through hole 1, then insert the tip of the needle in hole 2

Step 2 - As the needle goes into the fabric, pop the tip out at hole 3 (one square away from hole 1)

Step 3 - Pull the needle through to complete the stitch

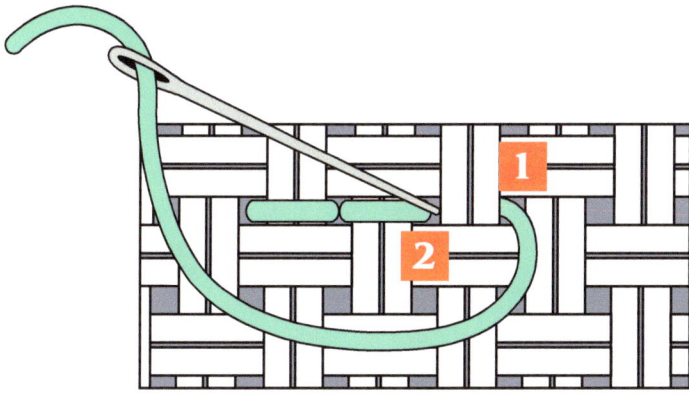

Step 1

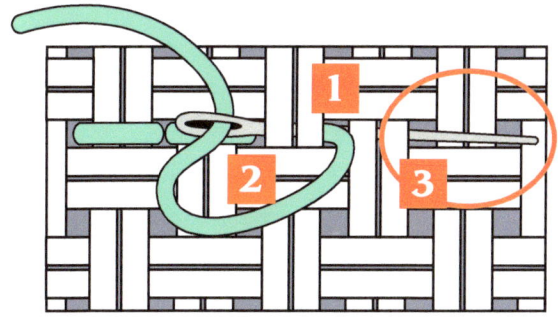

Step 2

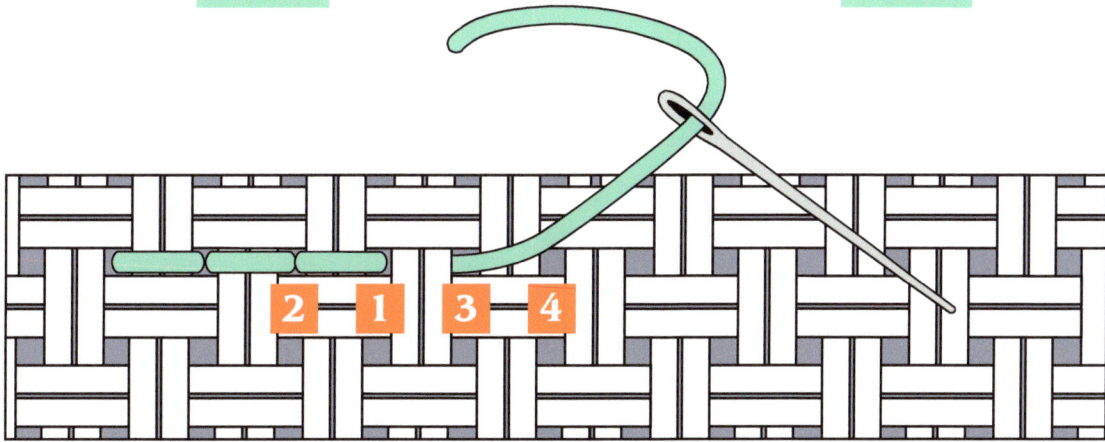

Step 3

To continue, you would then insert the tip of the needle in hole 1, pop the tip out at hole 4, and pull the thread through again, and so on. I think of it as "you come out ahead, but go in behind." So long as you're popping the needle tip out in the next empty square, and then going back in the previous hole to finish the stitch, it'll work out. Backstitching can take a while, but the results are definitely worth it!

Welcome to my world of Coloring & Cross-Stitch!

An Amazon bestseller & Book of the Month Club's Crafter's Choice!

Cross-stitch is a traditional hobby - but your designs don't have to be! These **more than 130 patterns** reflect a modern sensibility, with motifs ranging from trendy to vintage to kitschy, so there's something here for everyone. All are designed to fit into a 6-inch hoop or smaller, great for quick projects. Available in paperback and Kindle.

https://tinyurl.com/celtic-cross-stitch

A bestselling Celtic coloring book on Amazon!

50 pages of Celtic mandalas, designed to delight and inspire! With detailed artwork woven with Celtic knots and patterns, each page is perfect for relaxation and meditation, with a wide array of coloring inspiration to fit every mood and engage at every skill level.

https://tinyurl.com/celtic-mandalas

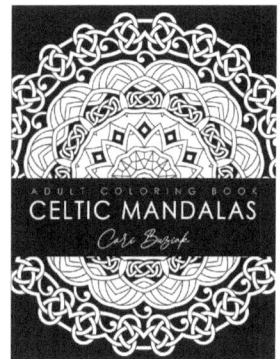

Are you a visual learner? Do you need to see the step-by-step in action for it to "click"? Then my YouTube channel is for you! Watch how-to videos, pick up tips & tricks, and download worksheets to practice your craft. **www.youtube.com/c/AonCelticArt**

Cari Buziak is a best-selling author and Celtic artist, known for her instructional books on calligraphy, cross-stitch, coloring, and Celtic art.

Visit her website **Aon-Celtic.com** to learn more!

Follow me @ aon-celtic.com!

etsy.com/shop/AonCelticArt   instagram.com/aoncelticart

facebook.com/AonCelticArt   pinterest.com/aoncelticart